Scroll Saw Silhouette Patterns

Patrick Spielman & James Reidle

Art by Dirk Boelman and Brian Dahlen

Sterling Publishing Co., Inc. New York

Library of Congress Cataloging-in-Publication Data

Spielman, Patrick E.
  Scroll saw silhouette patterns / by Patrick Spielman and James
    Reidle; art by Dirk Boelman and Brian Dahlen.
        p.   cm.
    Includes index.
    ISBN 0-8069-0306-6
      1. Jig saws.   2. Woodwork.   3. Silhouettes.   I. Reidle, James.
  II. Boelman, Dirk.   III. Dahlen, Brian.   IV. Title.
  TT186.S6743   1993
    684'.083—dc20   92-41352
                                                              CIP

Published by Sterling Publishing Company, Inc.
387 Park Avenue South, New York, N.Y. 10016
© 1993 by Patrick Spielman and James Reidle
Distributed in Canada by Sterling Publishing
c/o Canadian Manda Group, P.O. Box 920, Station U
Toronto, Ontario, Canada M8Z 5P9
Distributed in Great Britain and Europe by Cassell PLC
Villiers House, 41/47 Strand, London WC2N 5JE, England
Distributed in Australia by Capricorn Link Ltd.
P.O. Box 665, Lane Cove, NSW 2066
Manufactured in the United States of America
All rights reserved

Sterling ISBN 0-8069-0306-6

Preface

This book of silhouette patterns goes beyond the simple profiles of animals and the like. By and large, it also shies away from those exceedingly delicate and complex patterns requiring numerous small openings and inside cuts. The majority of patterns are essentially easy to moderately challenging; some are more detailed and fretted than others.

The book provides over 130 pattern designs in a variety of subject categories. The selection is sufficiently large and should satisfy a variety of interests. Some great sports scenes are included, which are perfect for decorating a young athlete's room (see Illus. 1). Animals, birds, and nautical designs can be used anywhere in the home. Nostalgic family and Victorian subjects are always a delight to make and are popular at craft shows. You will also find some humorous designs, a dragon (Illus. 2), cars, boats, and special Western, country, and Christmas themes. We've even included two silhouette patterns of people scroll-sawing.

We also discuss a variety of materials that can be used and the different ways that silhouettes can be mounted or displayed. Making silhouettes involves basic scroll-sawing skills, which almost anyone can learn and perfect quickly. The following information and tips may be beneficial to you, depending upon your previous scroll-sawing experience.

A number of helpful and creative individuals have contributed to the preparation of this book. We thank them for sharing their efforts and talents. First, we owe an enormous debt of appreciation to artist Brian Dahlen, who actually created most of the original designs, many of which are certain to become woodworking classics. Likewise, we express our gratitude to Dirk Boelman of The Art Factory and his assistant, Sharon Raines, for their original designs and precise tracings. We also thank Frank Joest for permitting us to convert two of his original paper-cutting designs into patterns for scroll sawing. And thanks, too, to the staff at Wildwood Designs, Richland Center, Wisconsin, developers and designers of fretwork patterns, for their overall assistance. We acknowledge with gratitude Delta International Machinery Corp. for allowing us to republish a number of classic silhouette scroll saw patterns, which appeared in early editions of the Rockwell/Delta DELTAGRAM™ Publication.

Thanks also to Sherri Valitchka and Jenny Blahnik for their computer work and thanks to our typist, Julie Kiehnau who, along with Karen Boelman, cut out cover samples and tested patterns.

Contents

Metric Equivalents

INCHES TO MILLIMETRES AND CENTIMETRES

MM—millimetres   CM—centimetres

Inches	MM	CM	Inches	CM	Inches	CM
⅛	3	0.3	9	22.9	30	76.2
¼	6	0.6	10	25.4	31	78.7
⅜	10	1.0	11	27.9	32	81.3
½	13	1.3	12	30.5	33	83.8
⅝	16	1.6	13	33.0	34	86.4
¾	19	1.9	14	35.6	35	88.9
⅞	22	2.2	15	38.1	36	91.4
1	25	2.5	16	40.6	37	94.0
1¼	32	3.2	17	43.2	38	96.5
1½	38	3.8	18	45.7	39	99.1
1¾	44	4.4	19	48.3	40	101.6
2	51	5.1	20	50.8	41	104.1
2½	64	6.4	21	53.3	42	106.7
3	76	7.6	22	55.9	43	109.2
3½	89	8.9	23	58.4	44	111.8
4	102	10.2	24	61.0	45	114.3
4½	114	11.4	25	63.5	46	116.8
5	127	12.7	26	66.0	47	119.4
6	152	15.2	27	68.6	48	121.9
7	178	17.8	28	71.1	49	124.5
8	203	20.3	29	73.7	50	127.0

Basic Techniques and Tips

Materials. A wide variety of materials can be used to make silhouettes, ranging from thick paper to many different wood materials, to soft metals and plastics. Typically, everyone first thinks of silhouettes as profile pictures cut from thin black material. To make these traditional-looking silhouettes, use thick black tag board. Even better, use ⅟₁₆- to ⅛-inch-thick Baltic birch or similar plywood. **TIP:** First spray-paint the plywood surfaces flat black with an aerosol before applying the pattern and sawing. Leave the sawn edges unpainted to contrast and emphasize the relief shadows. In like manner, you may opt to prestain the surfaces a color that contrasts with the material's color,

leaving the sawn edges unfinished. These are effective and interesting methods and they make finishing extremely simple.

Projects that are to be hung or mounted on dark backgrounds look best made from light, natural woods that are given clear finishes or simply left unfinished (see Illus. 1). Actually, we often prefer unfinished Baltic birch, placed against darker backgrounds, for many of the silhouette projects. Plywood is also often a good choice for strength reasons, because many of the patterns if cut from solid wood will have a short grain and will be very brittle in those areas (see illus. 1 to 4).

Even though plywood is always stronger than

Illus. 1. This silhouette is sawn from ⅜-inch or 7-ply Baltic birch plywood and left unfinished. Plywood is also a good choice because of its strength. (Pattern on page 109.)

Illus. 2. Some designs are visually impressive when sawn from thick solid woods. (Pattern on page 80.)

Illus. 3. An example of fragile, short-grain areas of a solid wood cutout.

solid wood, sometimes it's worth sacrificing strength for visual appeal. The dragon design in Illus. 2 looks great when cut from thin plywoods (up to ¼-inch thick), but would be considerably less appealing if cut from ¾-inch-thick plywood. However, when cut from thick (¾-inch) solid wood, the design also looks good, even though it must be handled carefully because of its fragile areas of short grain (see Illus. 3). Thick plywoods as a rule do not saw easily, anyway. The many glue lines dull the blades quickly, and charring of sawn edges is very likely, as are other sawing imperfections.

Thin solid wood, which may be even more delicate and fragile than plywood, can be cut cleanly and gives perhaps the best overall look. Always try to orientate the grain of solid wood to the characteristics of the pattern, in order to take advantage of the wood's linear strength (see Illus. 3 and 4).

Consider using nonwood materials such as clear plastic (Illus. 5). Its natural response to light rays makes it look very dimensional. There are many kinds of plastics with which you can experiment: colored transparent, translucent, metallic, solid-colored, and mirrored plastics all make stunning silhouette projects. Handle and clean all plastics carefully—especially the mirrored types—to avoid accidental scratching. Acrylics are much more difficult to saw than the polycarbonate types of plastic. Clean, smooth saw cuts are essential; otherwise, the entire effect and the good features afforded by plastics are destroyed. Generally, plastics must be cut cool, which requires slow blade speeds. Test-cut any unfamiliar material you use before undertaking a major project. Sandwiching plastic or thin metals between cheap plywood for cutting usually helps.

Illus. 4. This delicate design is strongest in solid wood with the grain running vertically. (Pattern on page 95.)

Illus. 5. This striking silhouette is cut from ¼-inch-thick polycarbonate plastic. Various light reflections make it look multi-dimensional. (Pattern on page 106.)

Transferring Patterns. Transferring patterns to material for sawing can be done in traditional ways, such as tracing with copy papers (carbon or graphite). However, the new, faster techniques involve: (1) copying the pattern directly from the book on an office copy machine, at which time it can be enlarged or reduced if desired, and (2) coating the back of the pattern with a very light mist of special spray adhesive (Illus. 6) and simply hand-pressing the paper pattern copy directly onto the work piece. Temporary bonding spray adhesives are available from craft shops and mail order sources. One kind we use is 3-M's Scotch Brand Spray Mount Adhesive, but other brands work equally well. Test the adhesive on scrap first before using. To use the spray adhesive, simply spray a very light mist onto the back of the pattern copy—

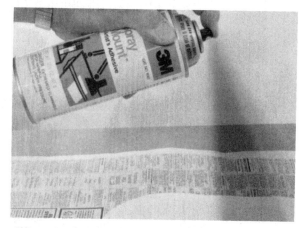

Illus. 6. Spray a light mist of special temporary bonding adhesive onto the back of the paper pattern. Note the newspaper below to catch the overspray.

do not spray it on the wood. Wait 10–30 seconds, and press the pattern onto the work piece. It should maintain contact during sawing. After all the cutting is completed, the paper pattern should peel very easily and cleanly from the work piece without effort, as shown in Illus. 7. Should the pattern be difficult to remove because too much adhesive was used, simply wipe the top of the pattern with a rag that has been slightly dampened in solvent.

Veining. This is a sawing technique specified on many patterns to make them appear more realistic and detailed. Veining is the technique of making a single kerf or interior saw cut (illus. 8 and 9) through the work to represent a certain feature or effect. A vivid example is making single line cuts in a leaf to represent its veins. Veining of sawn leaf designs was widely employed by scroll sawyers over a hundred years ago, and from those designs this technique got its name. Veining lines can originate entirely within the design itself or be cut by sawing inward from the outside edge.

Normally, veining is done with fine, thin blades, but the actual size used depends upon the material thickness and the character of the line being cut. Interior veining is most effective when the blade entry hole is barely large enough to permit the blade to be threaded through the workpiece. A $\frac{3}{64}''$-diameter hole will allow the use of a #4 scroll/fretsaw blade. A $\frac{1}{32}''$-diameter hole allows a #2 blade. If the material is very thin, use a sharp knife to make a very narrow, undetectable slit for blade entry. **TIP:** Sharpen the end of the blade to a point so it can be forced into a hole that is smaller than the usual size, to make the blade threading area almost totally undetectable.

Stack Sawing. Stack sawing is a basic production technique that should not be overlooked (see Illus. 10). It involves sawing two or more layers of material at the same time. By sawing multiple layers all at once, you obviously increase output. Sometimes scroll sawyers will use a cheap, low-grade material as a bottom

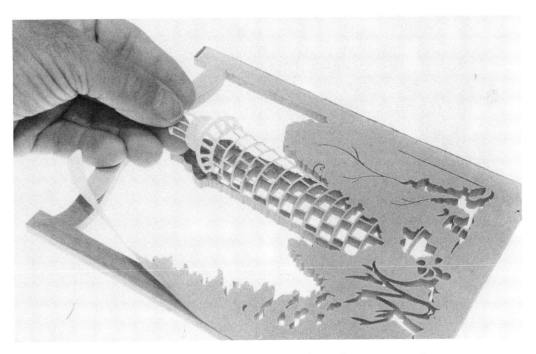

Illus. 7. Peeling the paper pattern from the sawn workpiece.

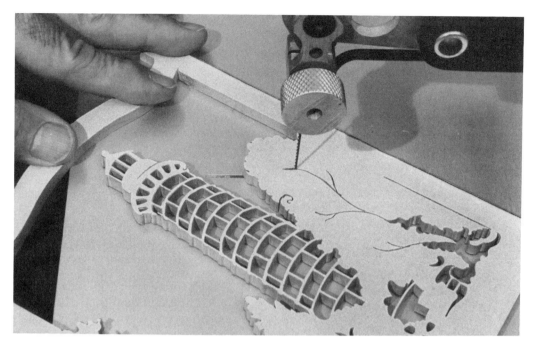

Illus. 8. Making single kerf veining cuts adds detail and visual interest to many cutouts.

Illus. 9. This design exploits the use of veining cuts to show the folds in the uniform, head details, etc. (Pattern on page 97.)

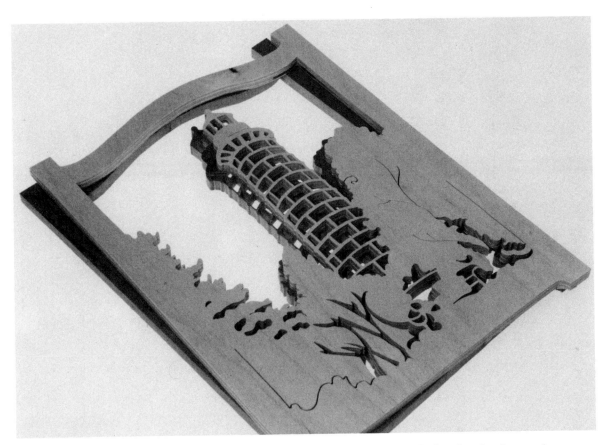

Illus. 10. Stack sawing produces identical pieces. Here Baltic birch plywood and solid mahogany were cut at the same time, one layered over the other.

layer to prevent saw blade tear-out or feathering from occurring on the bottom or exit side of the project itself. Layers can be held together in various ways while they are sawn, including nailing or tacking and spot gluing in the waste areas and using double-faced tape.

Displaying and Mounting Silhouettes.
There are many ways to utilize the silhouettes, other than just displaying the simple cutouts. Most are hung on the wall or are fitted into special, grooved blocks, and placed on mantelpieces and shelves.

Some designs can be backlit and used as night lights or seasonal decorations, as shown by the sample in illus. 11, 12, and 13. Thin plywood silhouettes can be glued to white or translucent colored plastic using a good spray adhesive. A 7½-watt bulb provides sufficient light. The socket and cord shown in Illus. 12 is available from some hardware stores or may be ordered from Wildwood Designs, Box 661, Richland Center, Wisconsin 53581.

Silhouettes can also be used as permanent

Illus. 11. Front view of a silhouette mounted onto translucent plastic and back lit. (Pattern on page 28.)

Illus. 12. Rear view of Illus. 11 shows the base and a socket with a 7½-watt bulb.

Illus. 13. Silhouette sawn from ¹⁄₁₆-inch Baltic birch plywood is mounted to ⅛" plastic with spray adhesive. Always test new adhesives on scrap.

overlays for jewelry-box covers, cabinet or furniture door fronts, or on architectural panels. They can be framed and backed with various fabrics, such as velvet or felt, which has been stretched over a panel. Tag board of a contrasting color to the silhouette (Illus. 14) and mirrored plastic (illus. 15, 16, and 17) make excellent backings, which give more visual interest and depth to the project.

Many silhouette designs can be adapted to incorporate battery-operated clocks or can become the basis for a sign for a family or business. To make a sign, do your silhouette on a piece of material with extra space on the bottom to accommodate a name of applied cutout letters or pierced letters.

Combining any of the previous ideas and engaging your own creative efforts will multiply the ways to profitably utilize the patterns and design ideas that follow.

Illus. 14. A silhouette mounted to tagboard and framed without glass. (Pattern on pages 112–113.)

Illus. 15. A silhouette with a mirrored plastic backing. (Pattern on page 142.)

Illus. 16. Another example of a mirrored plastic backing, attached to a ¼-inch-thick solid walnut silhouette. (Pattern on page 125.)

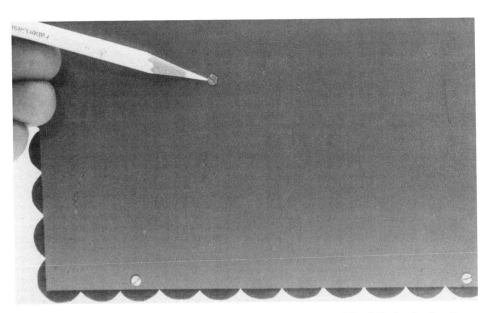

Illus. 17. Rear view of project shown in Illus. 16. The ⅛"-thick plastic mirror is fastened to the wood silhouette with a few small but strategically located wood screws.

Patterns

Birds

A

B

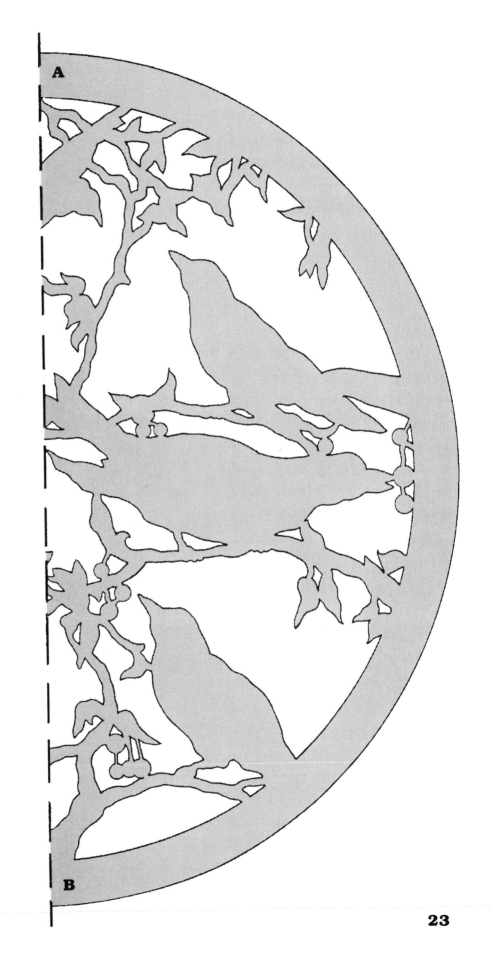

A

B

23

24

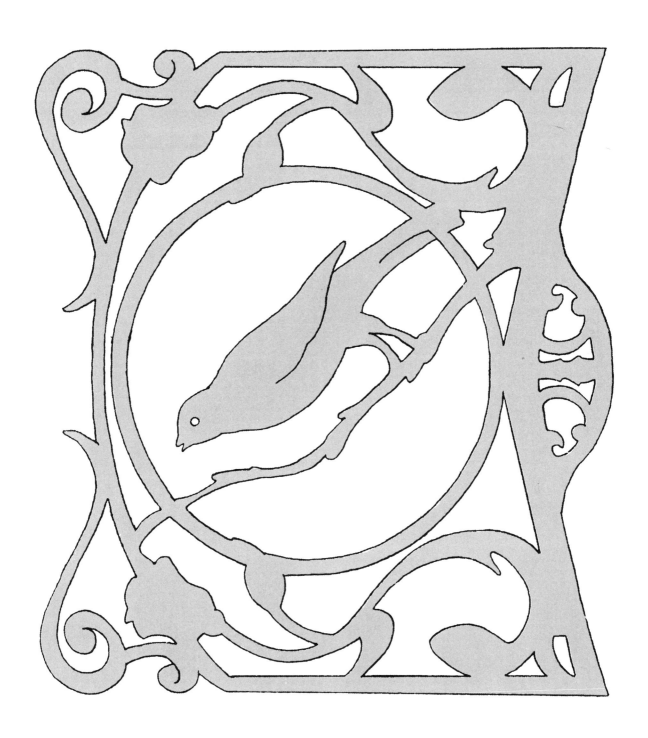

26

Other Animals

31

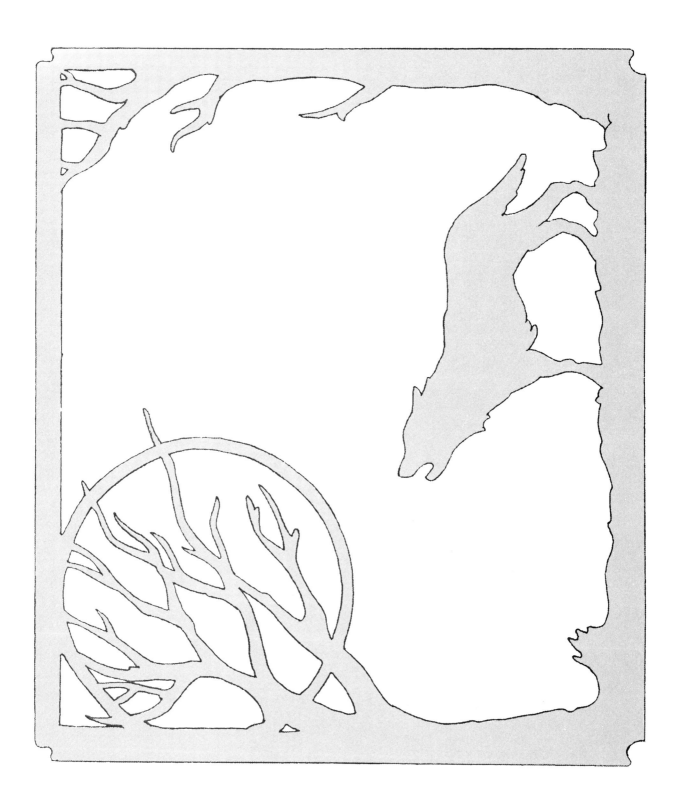

Pattern design courtesy Frank Joest.

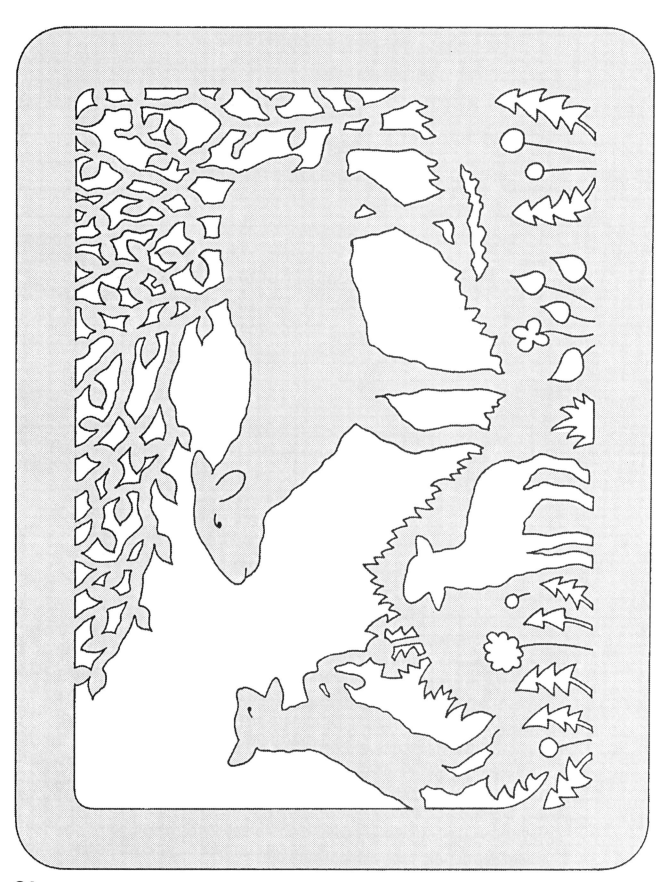

34

B

A

B

A

39

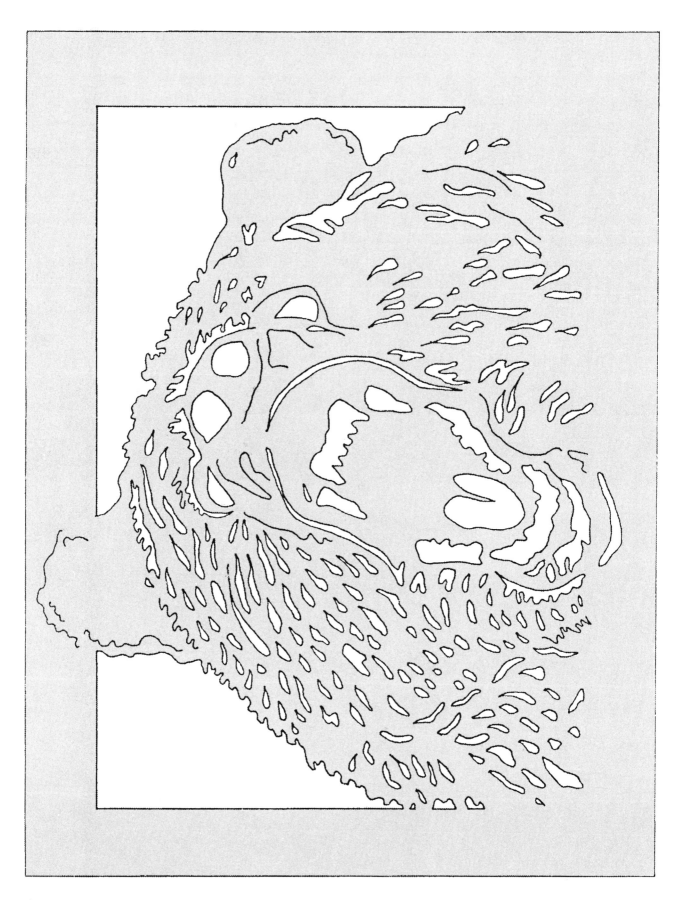

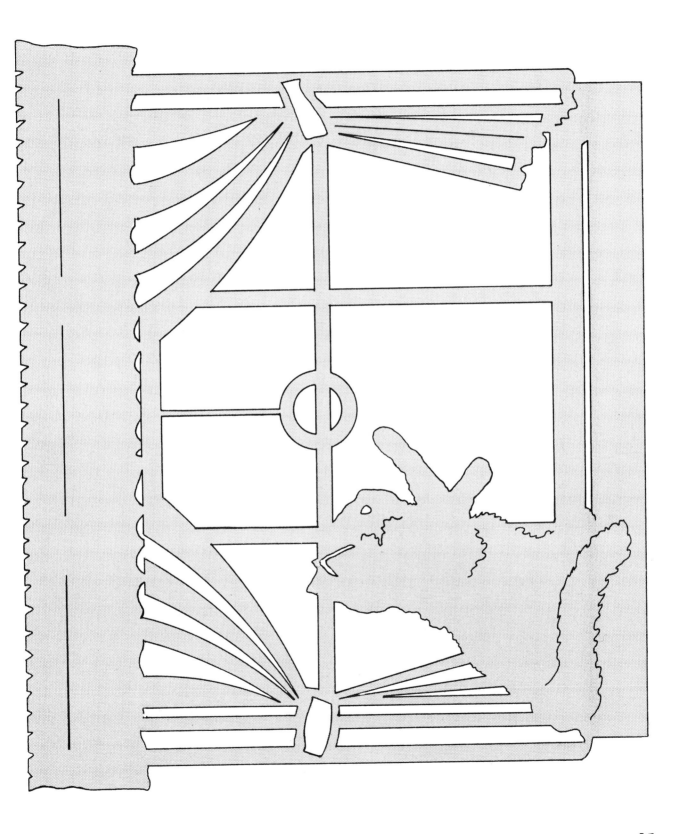

Christmas
and Easter

Pattern design courtesy Frank Joest.

A

B

44

A

B

45

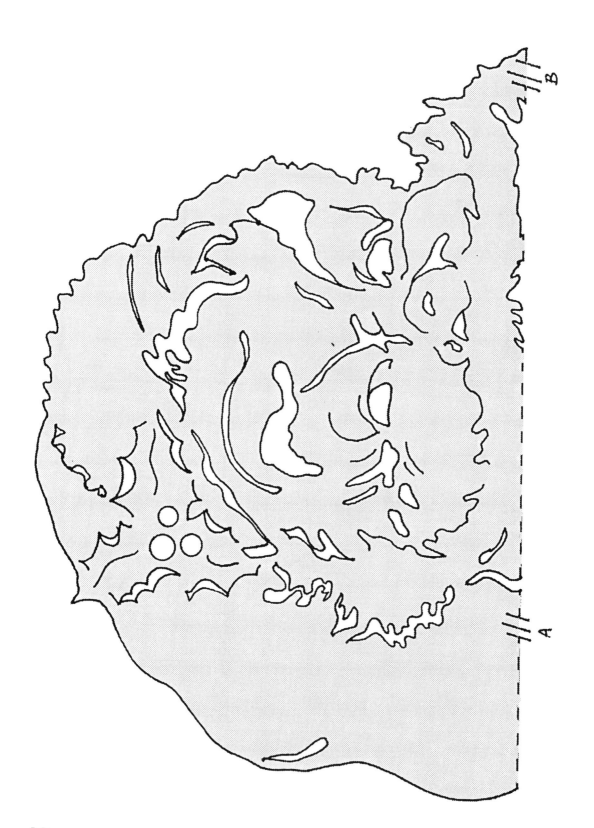

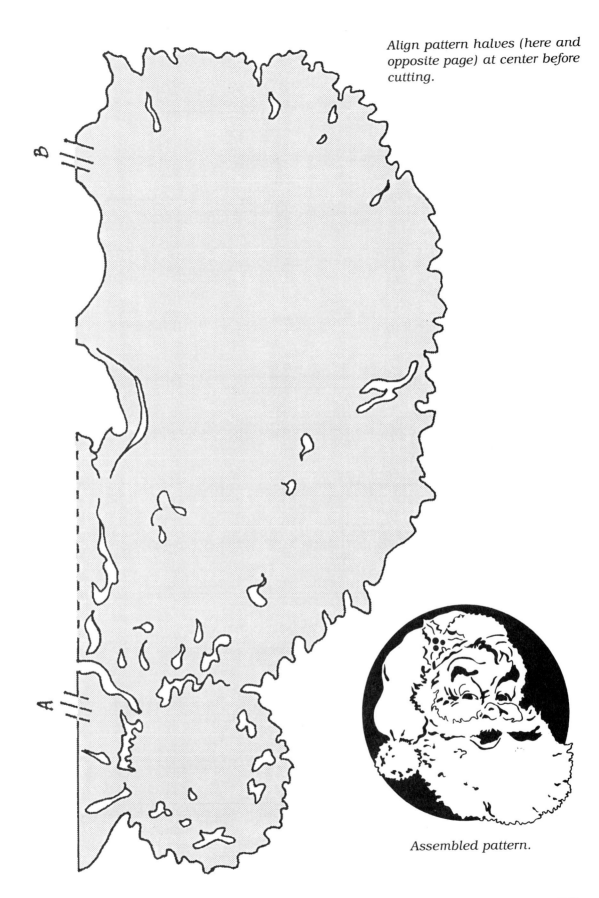

Align pattern halves (here and opposite page) at center before cutting.

B

A

Assembled pattern.

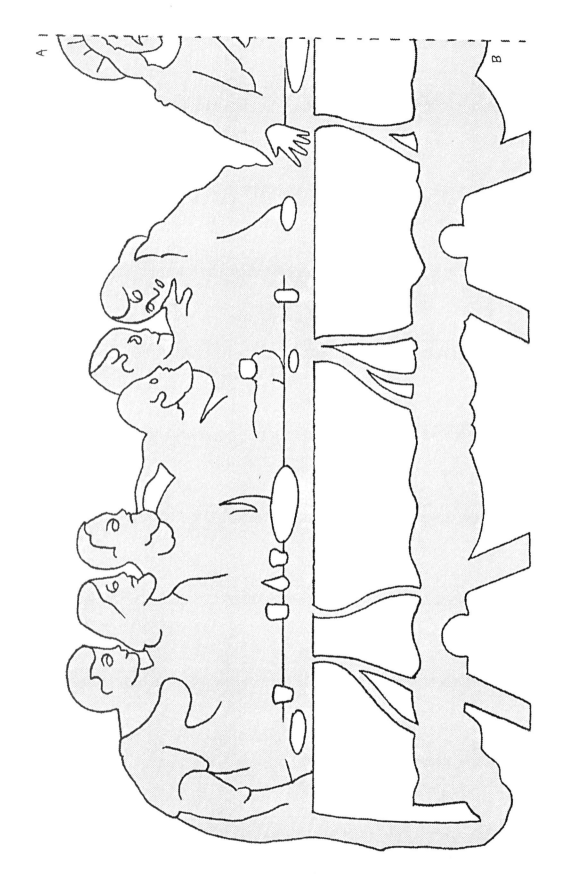

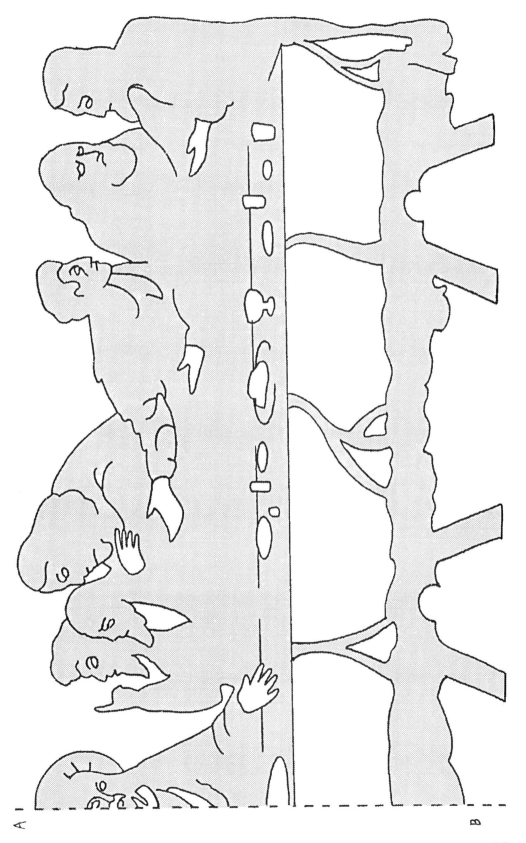

A

B

49

50

51

Country Scenes

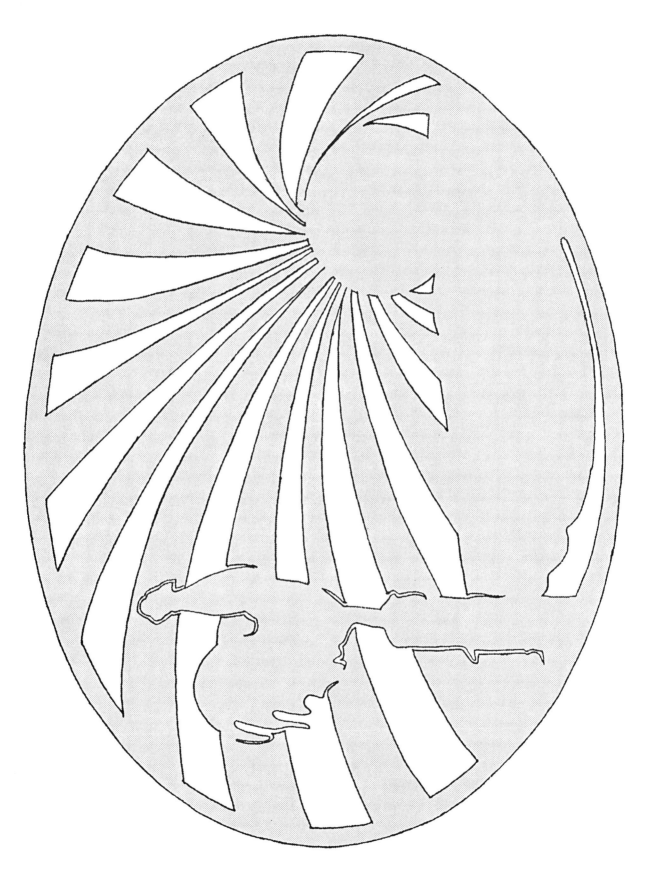

53

54

57

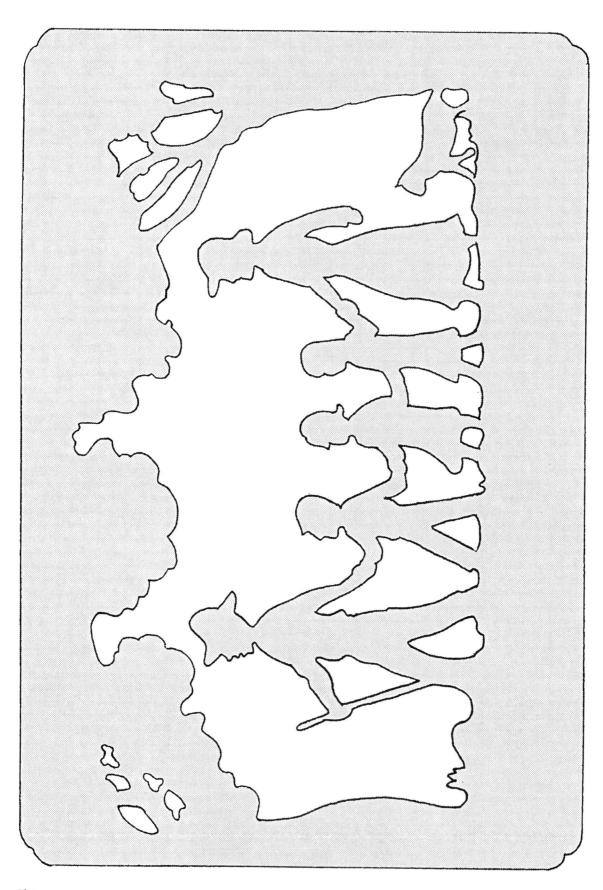

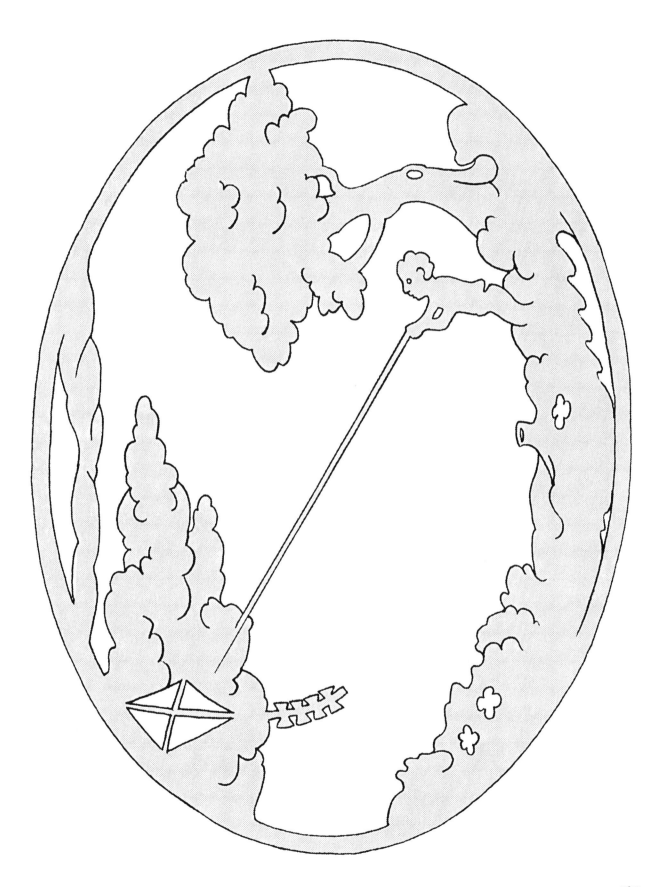

Family

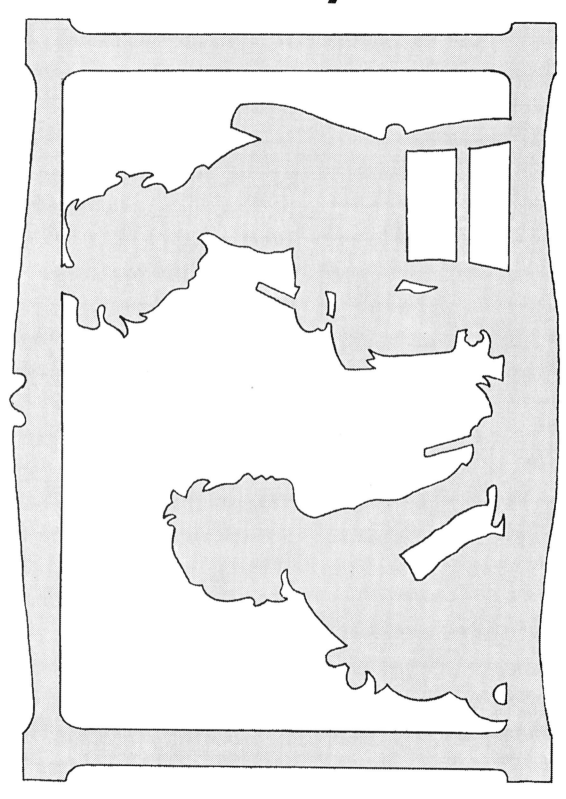

61

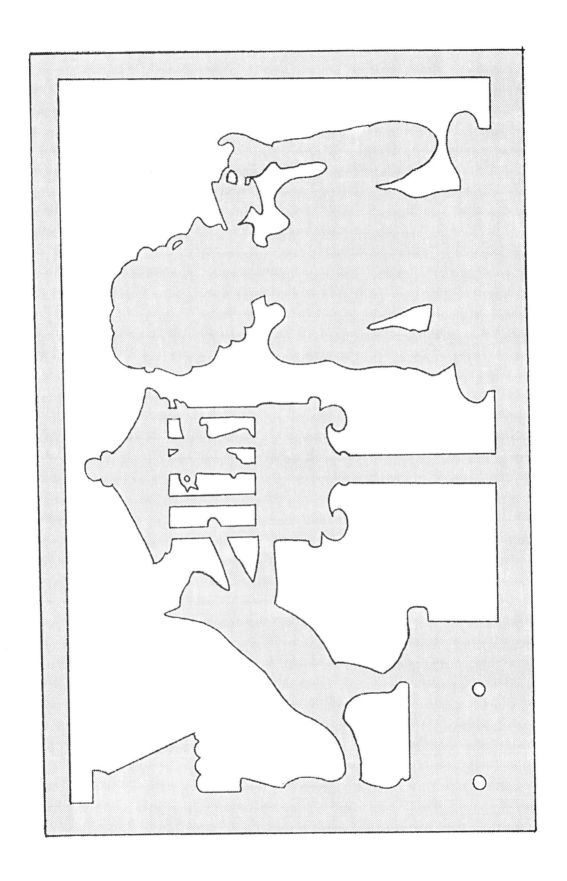

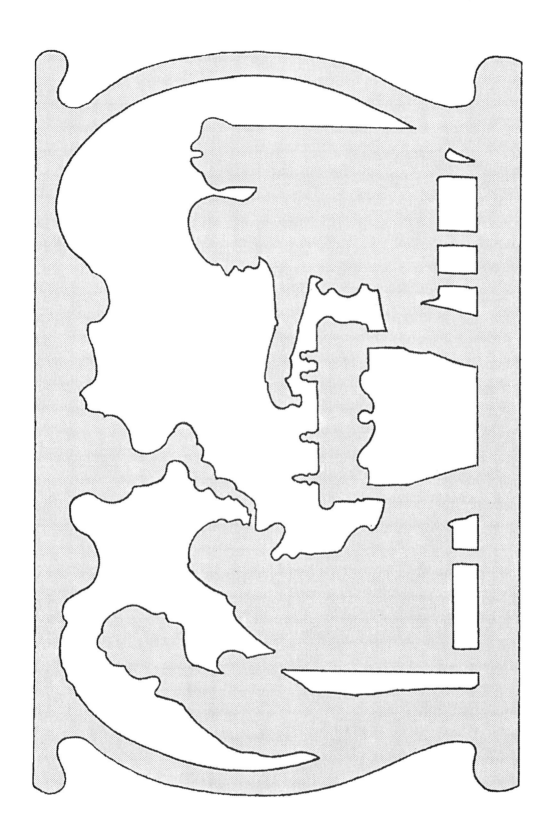

66

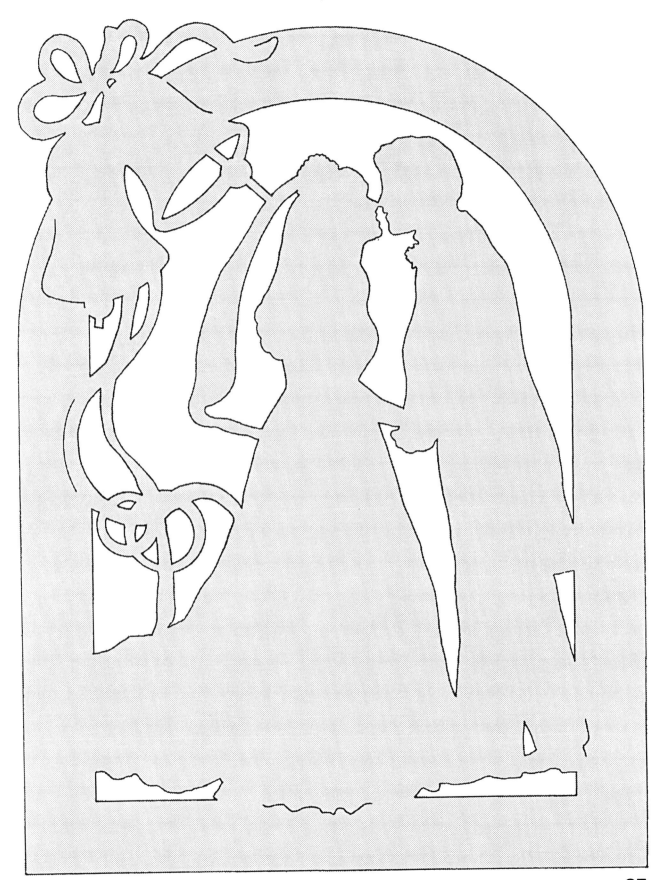

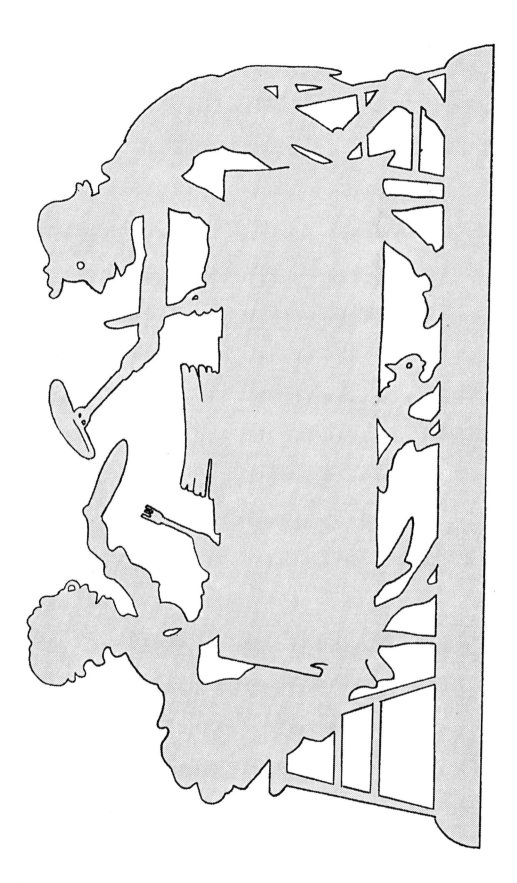

Field and Stream

70

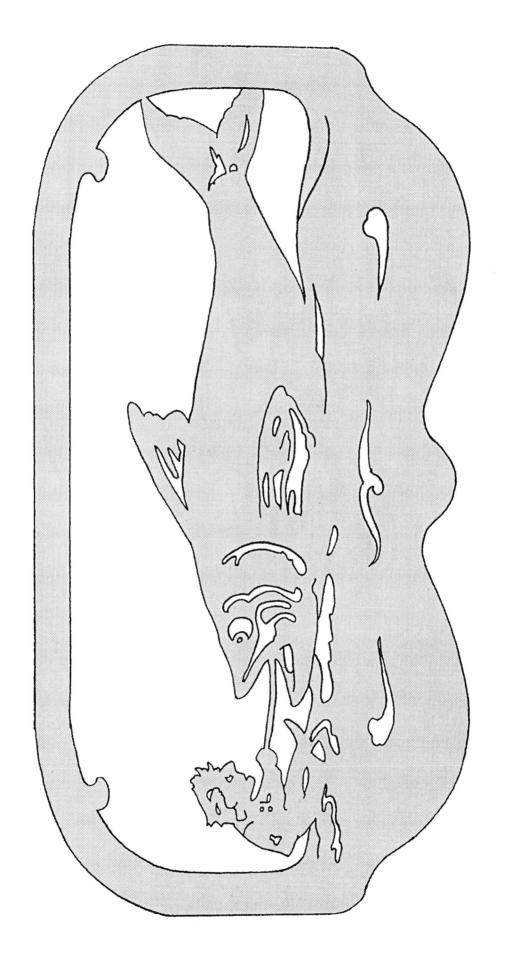

74

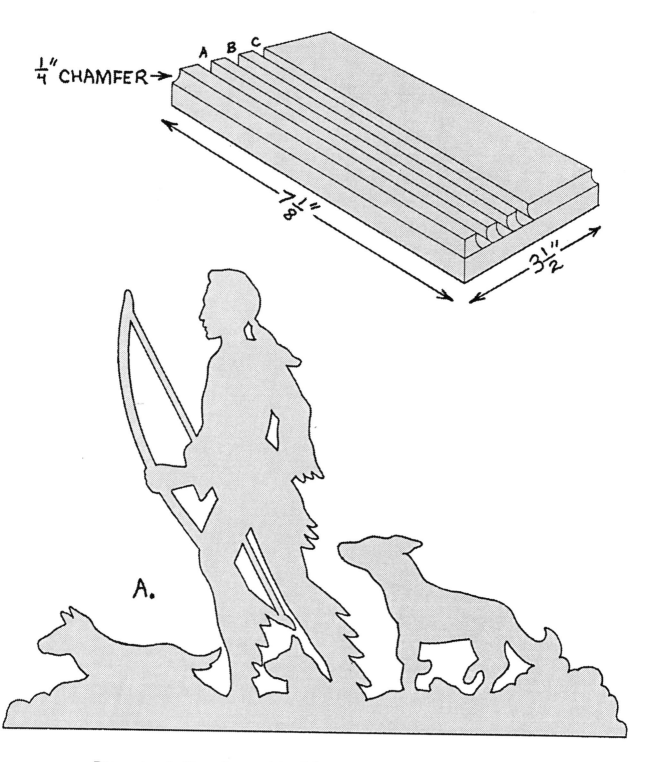

$\frac{1}{4}''$ CHAMFER →

A   B   C

$7\frac{1}{8}''$

$3\frac{1}{2}''$

A.

Dimensional silhouette consists of three pieces, A, B, and C. Part "C" may be made of plastic with a light behind it.

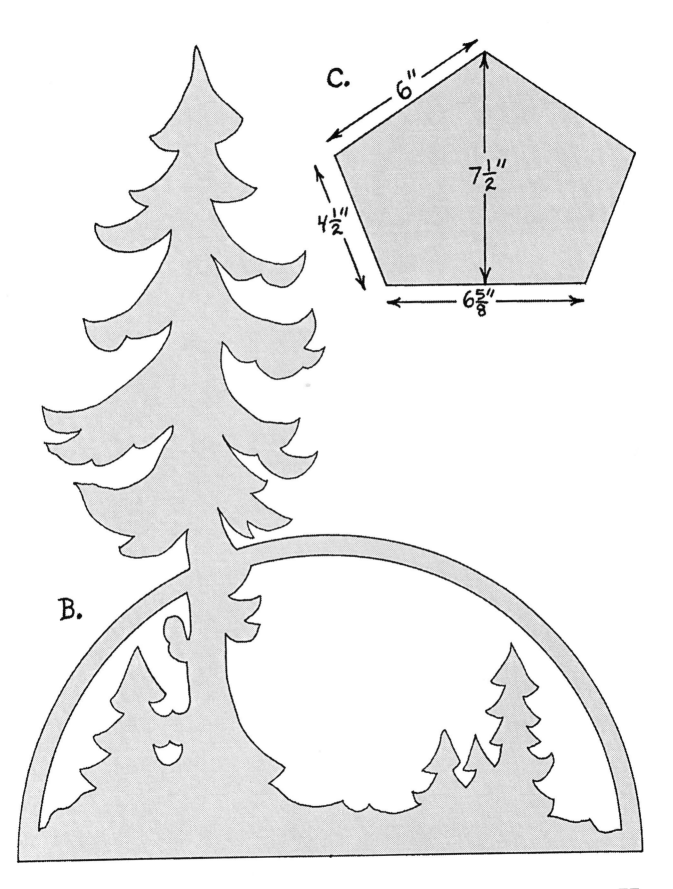

C.

6"

7$\frac{1}{2}$"

4$\frac{1}{2}$"

6$\frac{5}{8}$"

B.

77

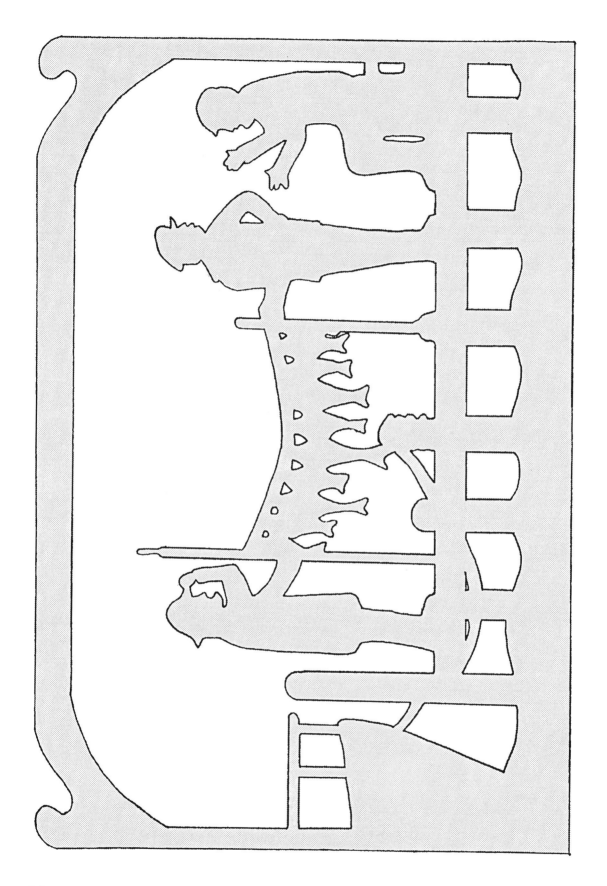

78

Mythology

80

81

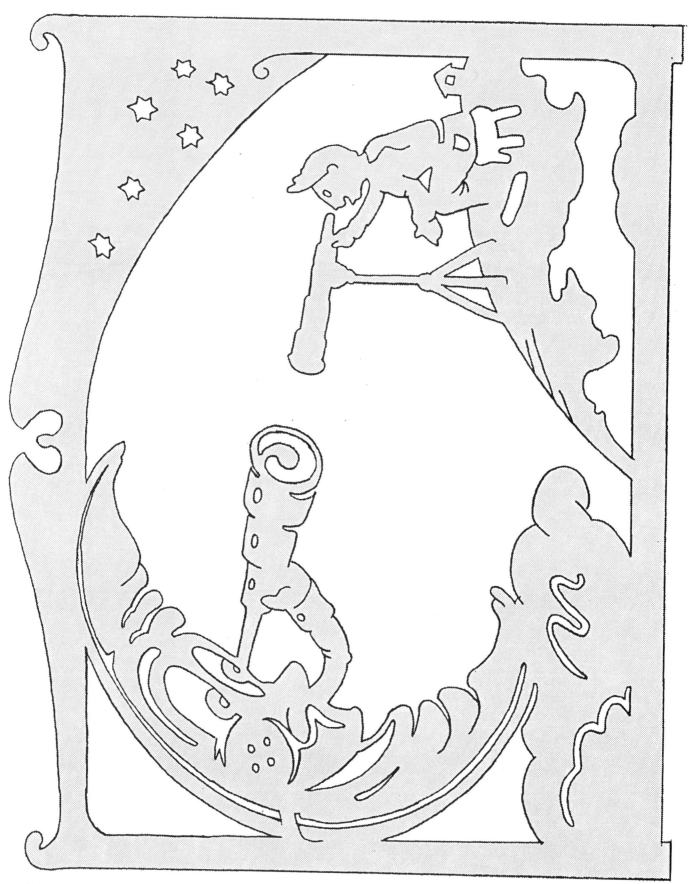

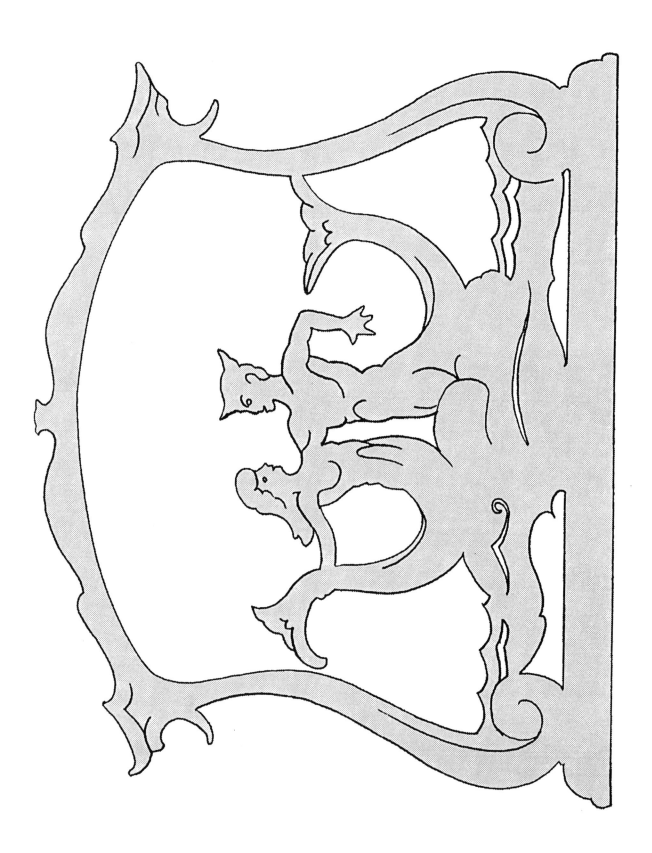

Nautical Scenes

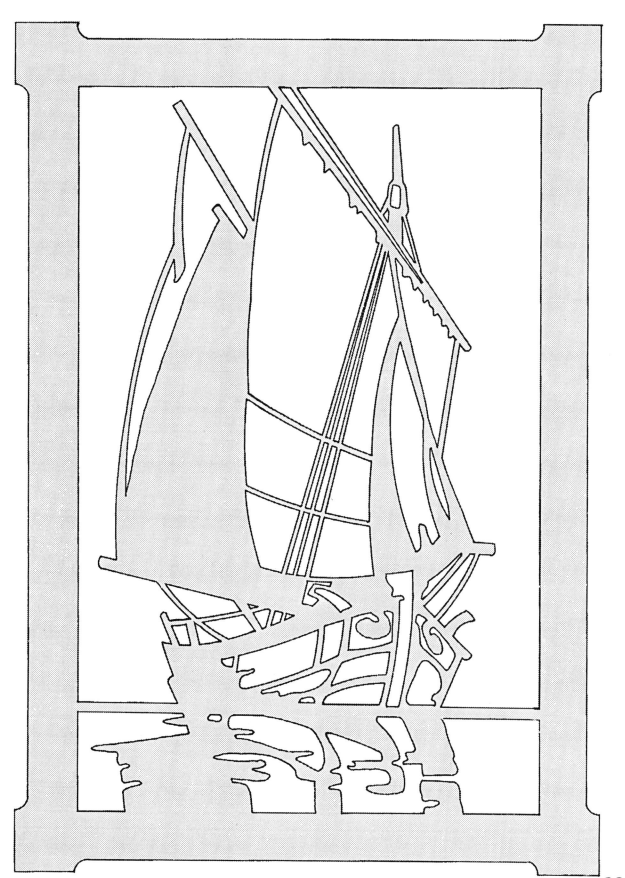

89

90

91

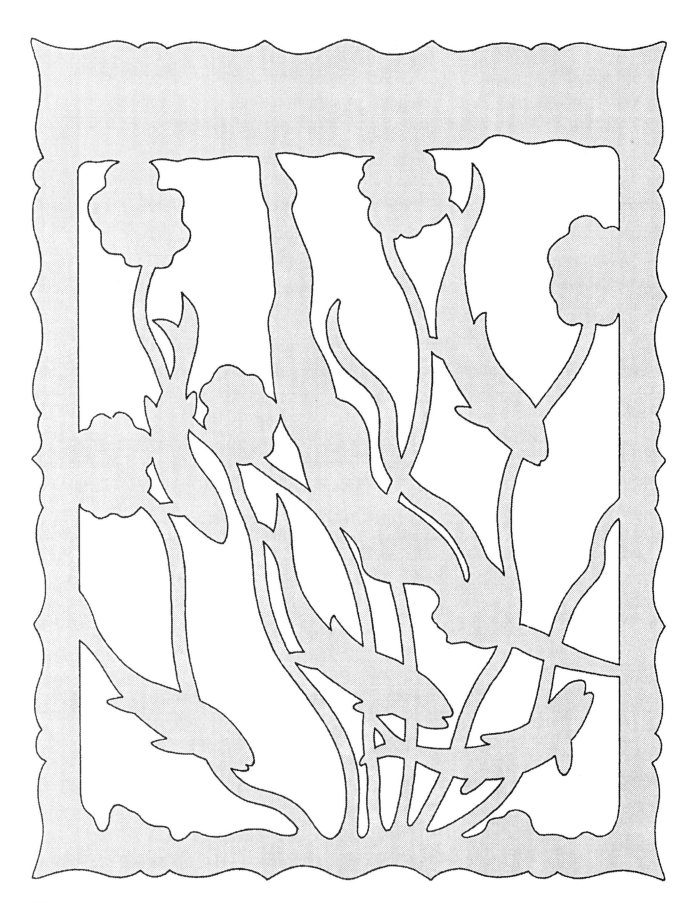

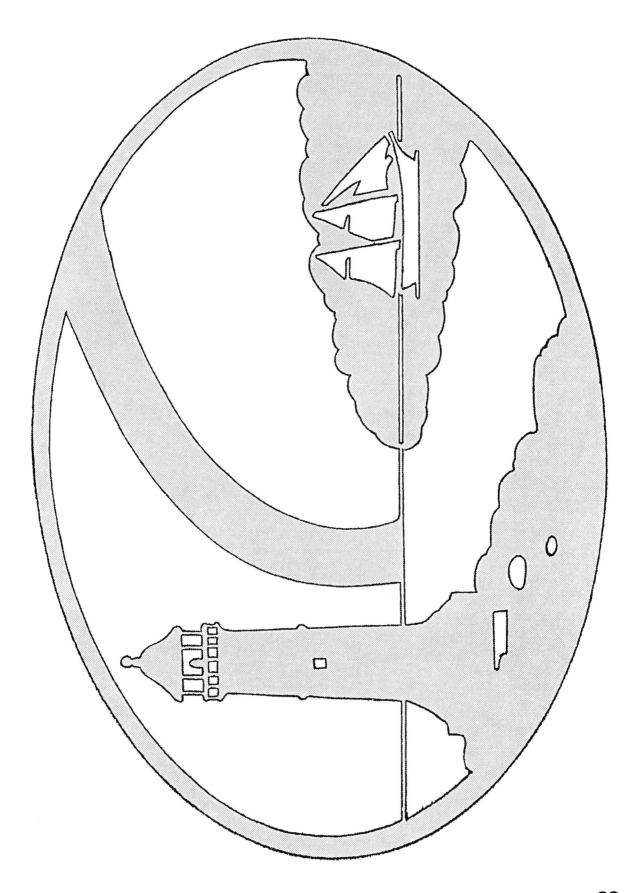

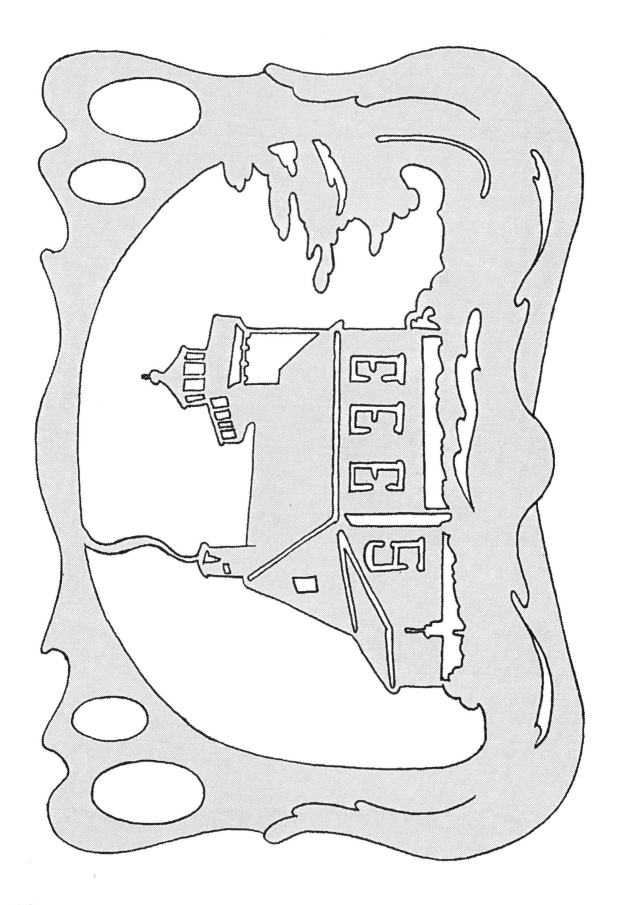

95

Sports

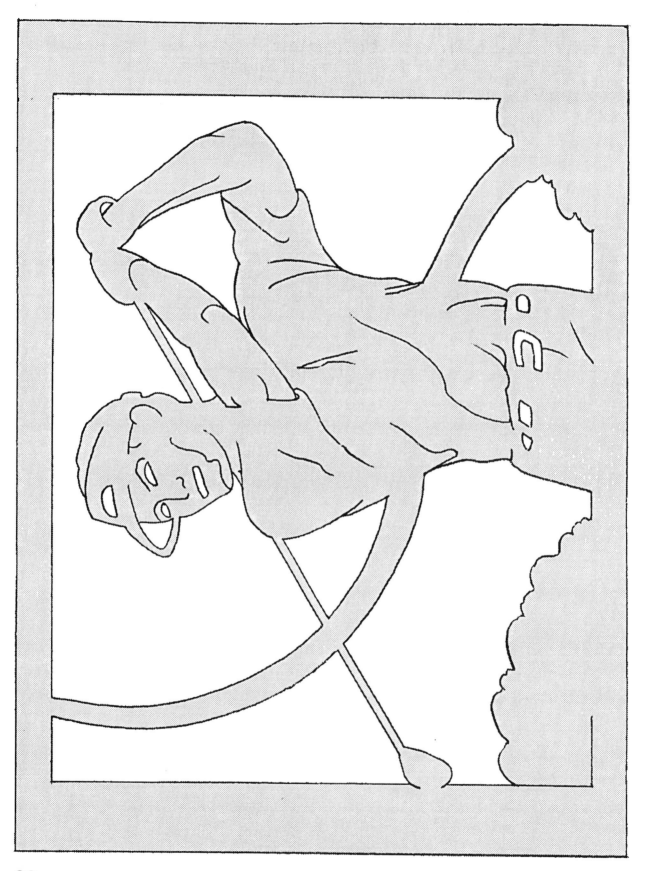

98

99

103

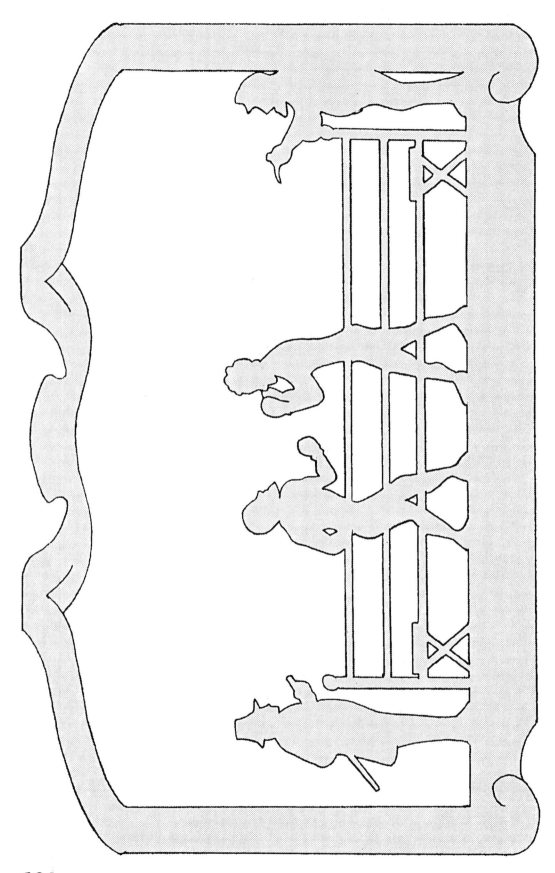

106

Transportation

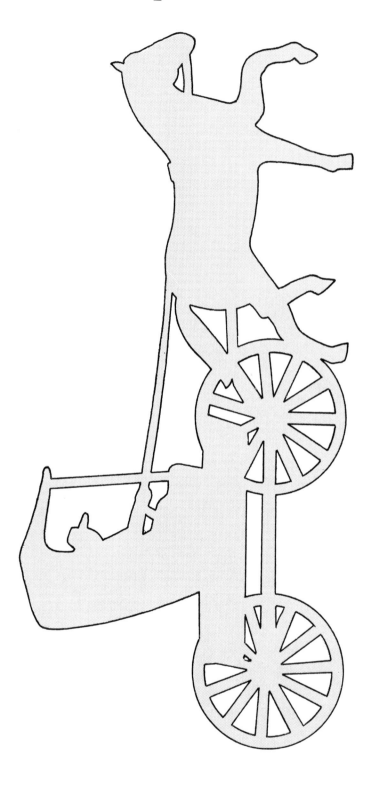

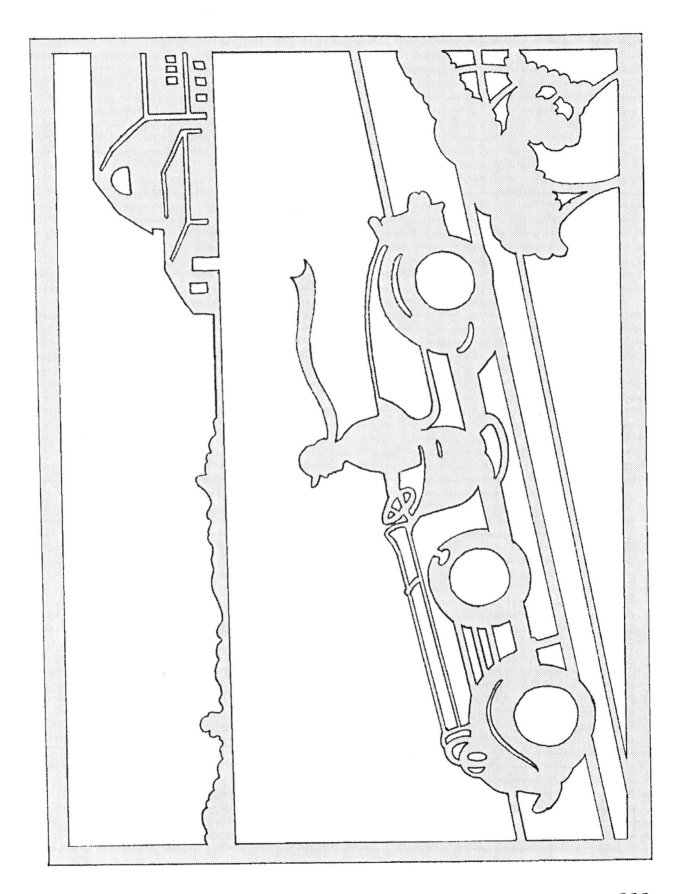

111

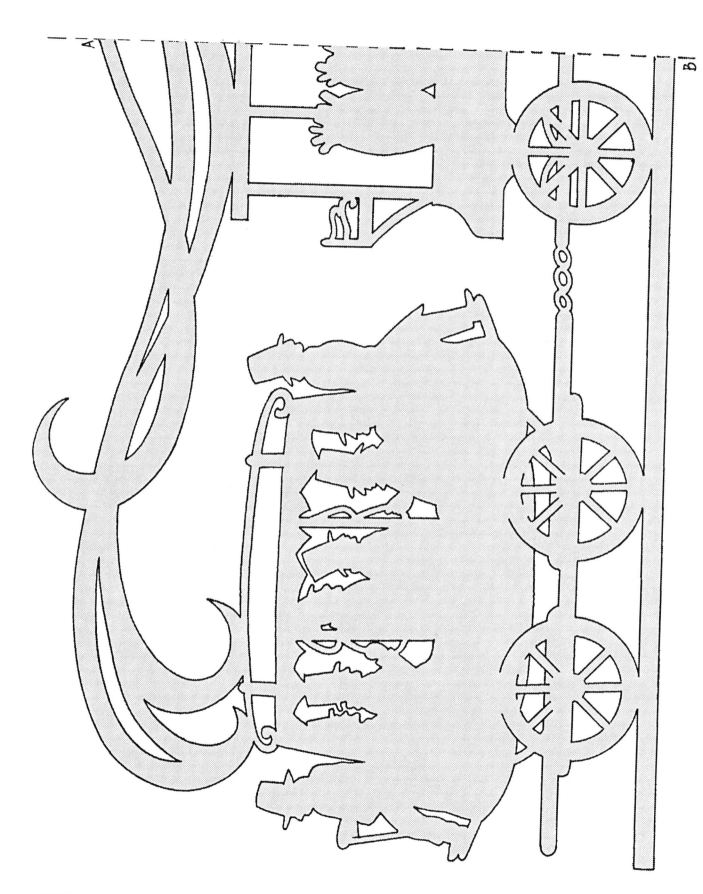

A

B

113

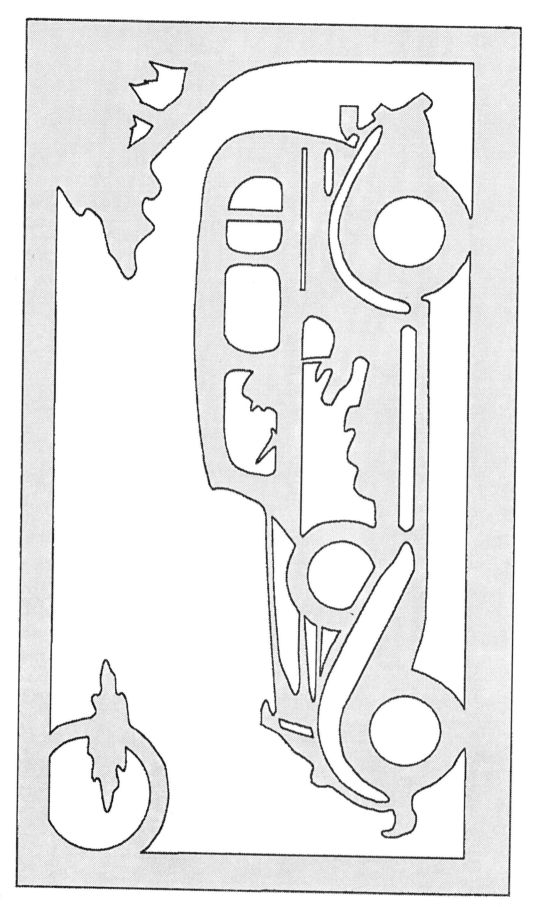

Victoriana

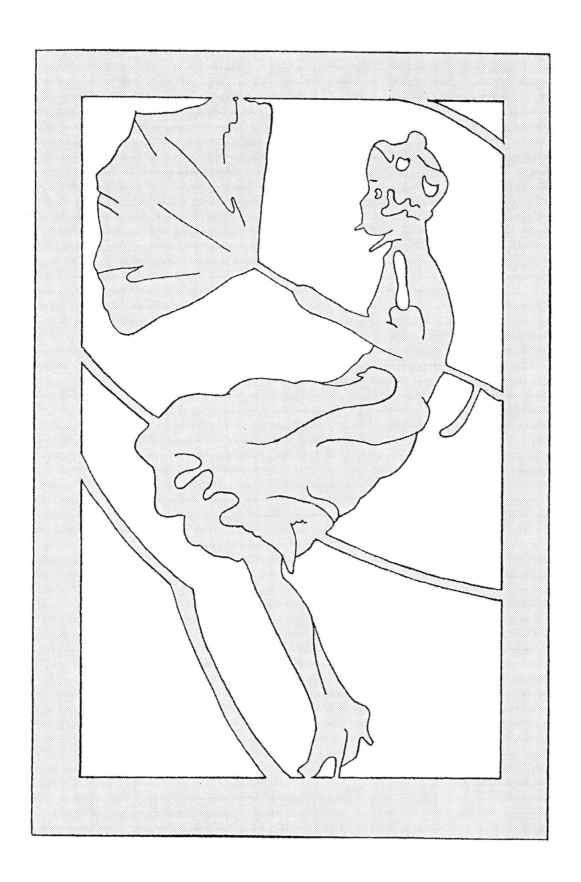

A

B

122

127

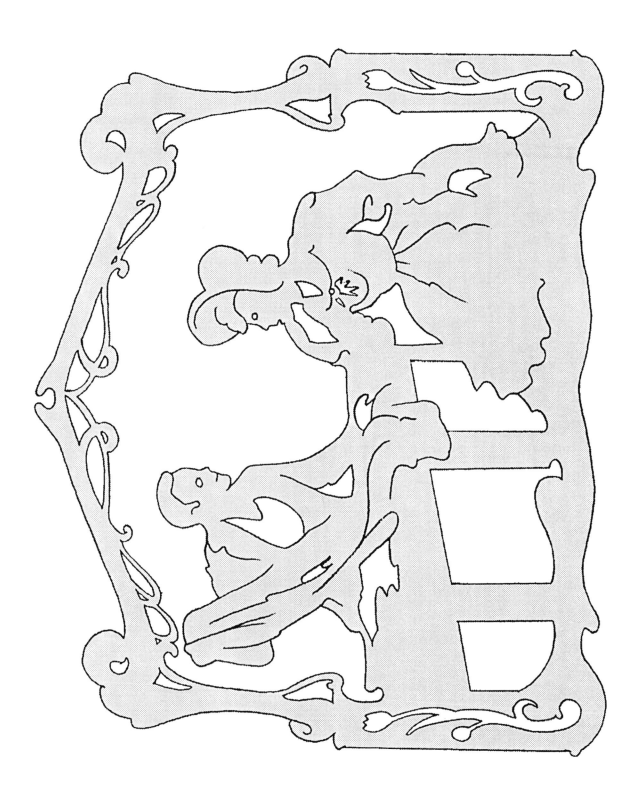

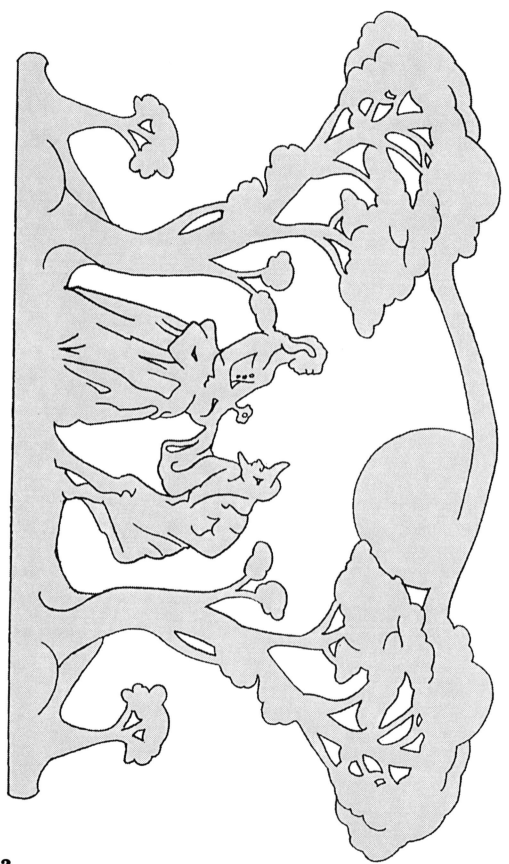

133

Warriors

137

138

Western Scenes

141

Winter Scenes

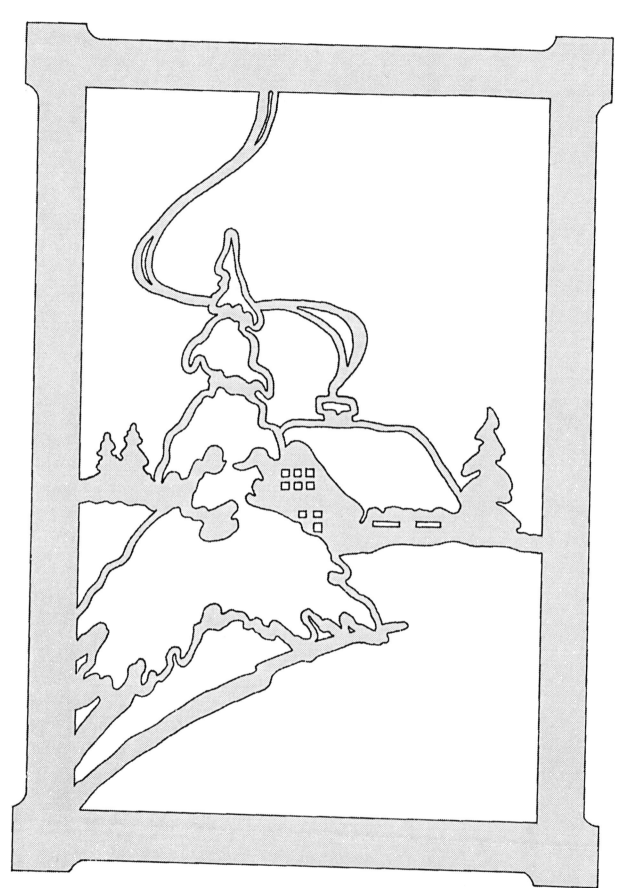

Miscellaneous

146

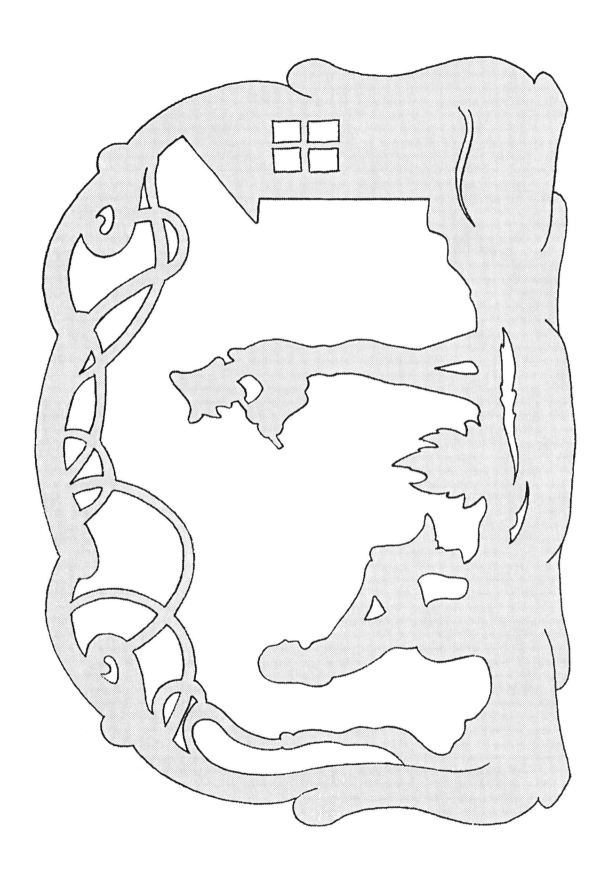

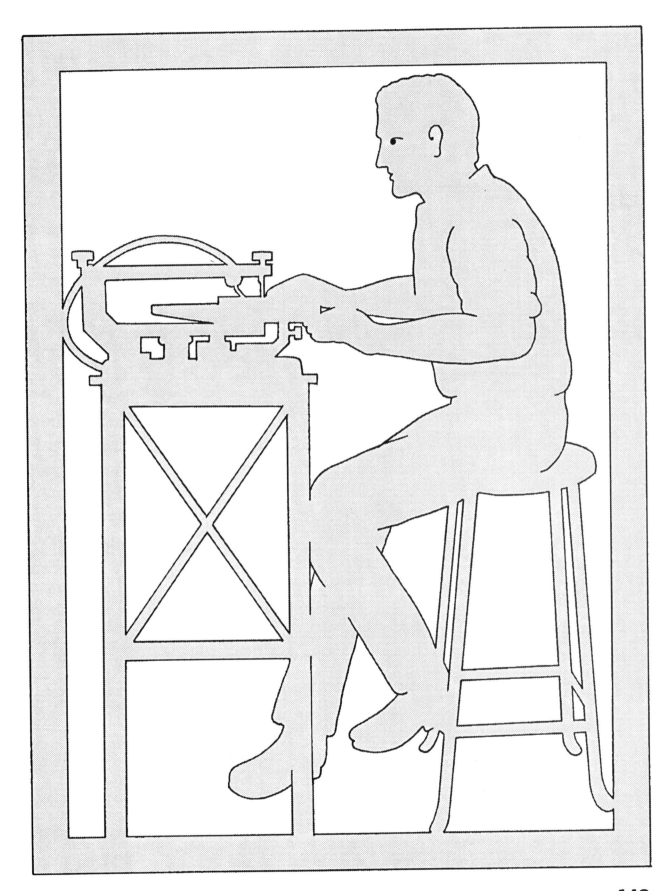

Design courtesy of Adolph Vandertie.

Design courtesy of Adolph Vandertie.

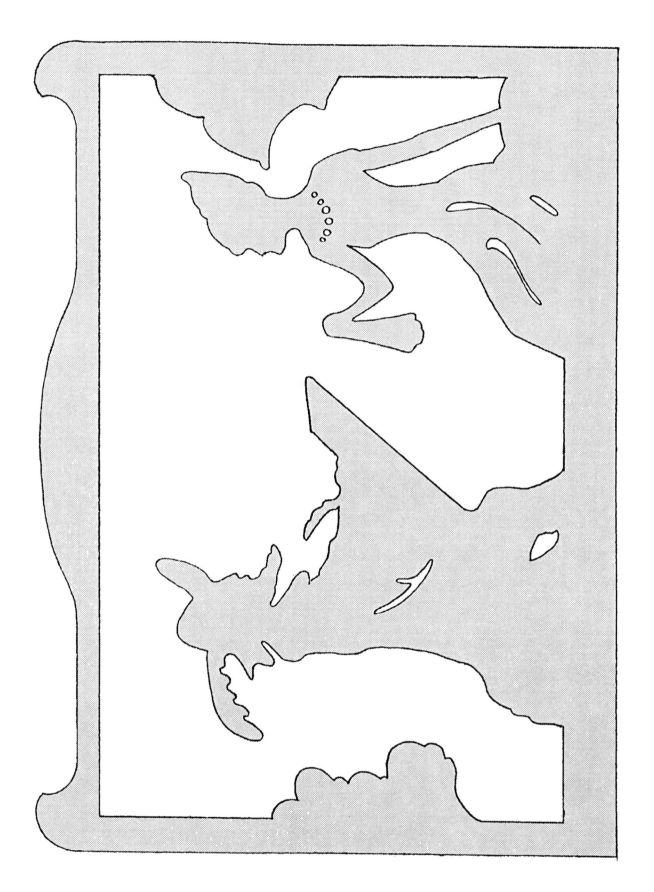

152

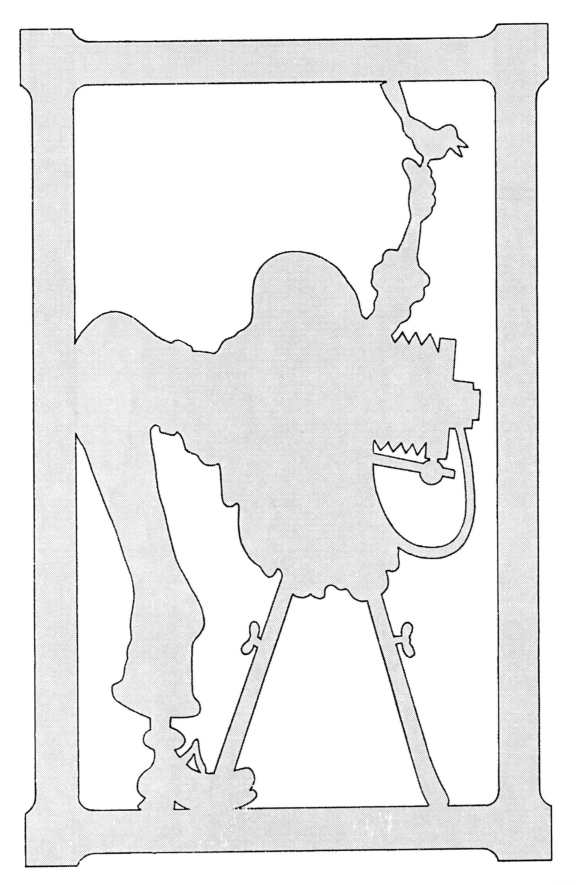

153

154

About the Authors

Patrick Spielman's love of wood began when, as a child, he transformed fruit crates into toys. Now this prolific and innovative woodworker is respected worldwide as a teacher and author.

His most famous contribution to the woodworking field has been his perfection of a method to season green wood with polyethylene glycol 1000 (PEG). He went on to invent, manufacture, and distribute the PEG-Thermovat chemical seasoning system.

During his many years as shop instructor in Wisconsin, Mr. Spielman published manuals, teaching guides, and more than 40 popular books, including *Modern Wood Technology*, a college text. He also wrote six educational series on wood technology, tool use, processing techniques, design, and wood-product planning.

Author of the best-selling *Router Handbook*, Mr. Spielman has served as editorial consultant to a professional magazine and as advisor and consultant to power tool manufacturers, and his products, techniques, and many books have been featured in numerous periodicals and on national television.

This pioneer of new ideas and inventor of countless jigs, fixtures, and designs used throughout the world is a unique combination of expert woodworker and brilliant teacher—all of which have endeared him to his many readers and to his publisher.

Co-author James Reidle has been doing fancy woodwook along with general carpentry all his life. He grew up watching his father create magnificent pieces of scroll-saw fretwork on treadle-type scroll saws. Years later, he wanted to recapture the best features of the early scroll saws his father used, so he developed one of his own, which is especially designed for fretwork and fine-detail scroll sawing. In addition, Reidle developed the first mail-order business in a number of years that is mainly devoted to fretwork patterns and supplies.

If you wish to contact the authors, send your correspondence to Sterling Publishing Co.

Current Books by Patrick Spielman

Carving Wild Animals: Life-Size Wood Figures. Spielman and renowned woodcarver Bill Dehos show how to carve more than 20 magnificent creatures of the North American wild. A cougar, black bear, prairie dog, squirrel, raccoon, and fox are some of the life-size animals included. Step-by-step, photo-filled instructions and multiple-view patterns, plus tips on the use of tools, wood selection, finishing, and polishing, help bring each animal to life. Oversized. Over 300 photos. 16 pages in full color. 240 pages.

Classic Fretwork Scroll Saw Patterns. Spielman and colleague James Reidle provide over 140 imaginative patterns inspired by and derived from mid- to late-19th-century scroll-saw masters. This book covers nearly 30 categories of patterns and includes a brief review of scroll-saw techniques and how to work with patterns. The patterns include ornamental numbers and letters, beautiful birds, signs, wall pockets, silhouettes, a sleigh, jewelry boxes, toy furniture, and more. 192 pages.

Country Mailboxes. Spielman and colleague Paul Meisel have come up with the 20 best country-style mailbox designs. They include an old pump fire wagon, a Western saddle, a Dalmatian, and even a boy fishing. Simple instructions cover cutting, painting, decorating, and installation. Over 200 illustrations. 4 pages in color. 160 pages.

Gluing & Clamping. A thorough, up-to-date examination of one of the most critical steps in woodworking. Spielman explores the features of every type of glue—from traditional animal-hide glues to the newest epoxies—the clamps and tools needed, the bonding properties of different wood species, safety tips, and all techniques from edge-to-edge and end-to-end gluing to applying plastic laminates. Also included is a glossary of terms. Over 500 illustrations. 256 pages.

Making Country-Rustic Wood Projects. Hundreds of photos, patterns, and detailed scaled drawings reveal construction methods, woodworking techniques, and Spielman's professional secrets for making indoor and outdoor furniture in the distinctly attractive Country-Rustic style. Covered are all aspects of furniture making from choosing the best wood for the job to texturing smooth boards. Among the dozens of projects are mailboxes, cabinets, shelves, coffee tables, weather vanes, doors, panelling, plant stands, and many other durable and economical pieces. 400 illustrations. 4 pages in full color. 164 pages.

Making Wood Bowls with a Router & Scroll Saw. Using scroll-saw rings, inlays, fretted edges, and much more, Spielman and master craftsman Carl Roehl have developed a completely new approach to creating decorative bowls. Over 200 illustrations. 8 pages in color. 168 pages.

Making Wood Decoys. A clear, step-by-step approach to the basics of decoy carving. This book is abundantly illustrated with close-up photos for designing; selecting, and obtaining woods; tools; feather detailing; painting; and finishing of decorative and working decoys. Six different professional decoy artists are featured. Photo gallery (4 pages in full color) along with numerous detailed plans for various popular decoys. 164 pages.

Making Wood Signs. Designing, selecting woods and tools, and every process through finishing clearly covered. Instructions for hand- and power-carving, routing, and sandblasting techniques for small to huge signs. Foolproof guides for professional letters and ornaments. Hundreds of photos (4 pages in full color). Lists sources for supplies and special tooling. 148 pages.

Original Scroll Saw Shelf Patterns. Patrick Spielman and Loren Raty provide over 50 original, full-sized patterns for wall shelves, which may be copied and applied directly to wood. Photographs of finished shelves are included, as well as information on choosing woods, stack sawing, and finishing. 4 pages in color. 132 pages.

Realistic Decoys. Spielman and master carver Keith Bridenhagen reveal their successful techniques for carving, feather texturing, painting, and finishing wood decoys. Details you can't find elsewhere—anatomy, attitudes, markings, and the easy, step-by-step approach to perfect delicate procedures—make this book invaluable. Includes listings for contests, shows, and sources of tools and supplies. 274 close-up photos. 8 pages in color. 232 pages.

Router Basics. With over 200 close-up, step-by-step photos and drawings, this valuable overview will guide the new owner, as well as provide a spark to owners for whom the router isn't the tool they turn to most often. Covers all the basic router styles, along with how-it-works descriptions of all the major features. Includes sections on bits and accessories, as well as square-cutting and trimming, case and furniture routing, cutting circles and arcs, template and freehand routing, and using the router with a router table. 128 pages.

Router Handbook. With nearly 600 illustrations of every conceivable bit, attachment, jig, and fixture, plus every possible operation, this definitive guide has revolutionized router applications. It begins with safety and maintenance tips, then forges ahead into all aspects of dovetailing, freehanding, advanced duplication, and more. Details for over 50 projects are included. 224 pages.

Router Jigs & Techniques. A practical encyclopedia of information, covering the latest equipment to use with the router, it describes all the newest commercial routing machines, along with jigs, bits, and other aids and devices. The book not only provides invaluable tips on how to determine which router and bits to buy, it explains how to get the most out of the equipment once it is bought. Over 800 photos and illustrations. 383 pages.

Scroll Saw Basics. This overview features more than 275 illustrations covering basic techniques and accessories. Sections include types of saws, features, selection of blades, safety, and how to use patterns. Half a dozen patterns are included to help the scroll saw user get started. Basic cutting techniques are covered, including inside cuts, bevel cuts, stack-sawing, and others. 128 pages.

Scroll Saw Country Patterns. With 300 full-size patterns in 28 categories, this selection of projects covers an extraordinary range, with instructions every step of the way. Projects include farm animals, people, birds, and butterflies, plus letter and key holders, coasters, switch plates, country hearts, and more. Directions are given for piercing, drilling, sanding, and finishing, as well as tips on using special tools. 4 pages in color. 196 pages.

Scroll Saw Fretwork Patterns. This companion book to *Scroll Saw Fretwork Techniques & Projects* features over 200 fabulous, full-size fretwork patterns. These patterns, drawn by James Reidle, include popular classic designs, plus an array of imaginative contemporary ones. Choose from a variety of numbers, signs, brackets, animals, miniatures, and silhouettes, and more. 256 pages.

Scroll Saw Fretwork Techniques & Projects. This companion book to *Scroll Saw Fretwork Patterns* offers a study in the historical development of fretwork, as well as the tools, techniques, materials, and project styles that have evolved over the past 130 years. Every intricate turn and cut is explained, with over 550 step-by-step photos and illustrations. Patterns for all 32 projects are shown in full color. The book also covers some modern scroll sawing machines as well as state-of-the-art fretwork and fine scroll-sawing techniques. 8 pages in color. 232 pages.

Scroll Saw Handbook. This companion volume to *Scroll Saw Pattern Book* covers the essentials of this versatile tool, including the basics (how scroll saws work, blades to use, etc.) and the advantages and disadvantages of the general types and specific brand-name models on the market. All cutting techniques are detailed, including compound and bevel sawing, making inlays, reliefs, and recesses, cutting metals and other nonwoods, and marquetry. There's even a section on transferring patterns to wood. Over 500 illustrations. 256 pages.

Scroll Saw Holiday Patterns. Patrick and Patricia Spielman provide over 100 full-size, shaded patterns for easy cutting, plus full-color photos of projects. This book will serve all holiday pleasures—all year long. Use these holiday patterns to create decorations, centerpieces, mailboxes, and diverse projects to keep or give as gifts. Standard holidays, as well as the four seasons, birthdays, and anniversaries, are represented. 8 pages of color. 168 pages.

Scroll Saw Pattern Book. This companion book to *Scroll Saw Handbook* contains over 450 patterns for wall plaques, refrigerator magnets, candle holders, pegboards, jewelry, ornaments, shelves, brackets, picture frames, signboards, and many other projects. Beginning and experienced scroll saw users alike will find something to intrigue and challenge them. 256 pages.

Scroll Saw Puzzle Patterns. 80 full-size patterns for jigsaw puzzles, standup puzzles, and inlay puzzles. With meticulous attention to detail, Patrick and Patricia Spielman provide instructions and step-by-step photos, along with tips on tools and wood selection, for making dinosaurs, camels, hippopotami, alligators—even a family of elephants! Inlay puzzle patterns include basic shapes, numbers, an accurate piece-together map of the United States, and a host of other colorful educational and enjoyable games for children. 8 pages of color. 264 pages.

Scroll Saw Shelf Patterns. Spielman and master scroll saw designer Loren Raty offer full-size patterns for 44 different shelf styles. Designs include wall shelves, corner shelves, and multi-tiered shelves. The patterns work well with 1/4-inch hardwood plywood or any solid wood. Over 150 illustrations. 4 pages in color. 132 pages.

Sharpening Basics. This overview goes well beyond the "basics," to become a major up-to-date reference work featuring more than 300 detailed illustrations (mostly photos) explaining every facet of tool sharpening. Sections include bench-sharpening tools, sharpening machines, and safety. Chapters cover cleaning tools, and sharpening all sorts of tools, including chisels, plane blades (irons), hand knives, carving tools, turning tools, drill and boring tools, router and shaper tools, jointer and planer knives, drivers and scrapers, and, of course, saws. 144 pages.

Spielman's Original Scroll Saw Patterns. 262 full-size patterns that don't appear elsewhere feature teddy bears, dinosaurs, sports figures, dancers, cowboy cutouts, Christmas ornaments, and dozens more. Fretwork patterns are included for a Viking ship, framed cutouts, wall-hangers, key-chain miniatures, jewelry, and much more. Hundreds of step-by-step photos and drawings show how to turn, repeat, and crop each design for thousands of variations. 4 pages of color. 228 pages.

Victorian Gingerbread: Patterns & Techniques. Authentic pattern designs (many full-size) cover the full range of indoor and outdoor detailing: brackets, corbels, shelves, grilles, spandrels, balusters, running trim, headers, valances, gable ornaments, screen doors, pickets, trellises, and much more. Also included are complete plans for Victorian mailboxes, house numbers, signs, and more. With clear instructions and helpful drawings by James Reidle, the book also provides tips for making gingerbread trim. 8 pages in color. 200 pages.

Victorian Scroll Saw Patterns. Intricate original designs plus classics from the 19th century are presented in full-size, shaded patterns. Instructions are provided with drawings and photos. Projects include alphabets and numbers, silhouettes and designs for shelves, frames, filigree baskets, plant holders, decorative boxes, picture frames, welcome signs, architectural ornaments, and much more. 160 pages.

Working Green Wood with PEG. Covers every process for making beautiful, inexpensive projects from green wood without cracking, splitting, or warping it. Hundreds of clear photos and drawings show every step from obtaining the raw wood through shaping, treating, and finishing PEG-treated projects. 175 unusual project ideas. Lists suppliers. 120 pages.

Index